Navika Deol
For you, who stole my heart

Illustrations by Julia Hann von Weyhern

The Book

It's just random poetry
written by me.
Especially 'bout love,
'bout desire,
'bout all the feelings connected to it.
Take your cup of tea and
just enjoy.
Let your senses fill up
with these trivial words.

The Author

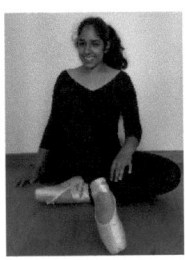

Navika Deol, born 1998 in Pforzheim, grew up with reading books and she published her first book "Gedankenverloren" in 2018. "For you, who stole my heart" is her first book completely written in English. She spends her free time with books, films and on her blog, which can be found in the internet at: www.szebrabooks.de.

The Illustrator

Julia Hann von Weyhern, born 2001 in Freiburg i. Br., studies communication design in Potsdam. Photography, art and poetry are essential to her as a creative being. The illustrations are partially visualised thought snippets of the poems and leave space for your own personal imagination.

For you, who stole my heart

Navika Deol

Illustrations by Julia Hann von Weyhern

Bibliographic information from the German National Library: The German National Library lists this publication in the German National Bibliography; detailed bibliographical data can be found on the internet at dnb.dnb.de

First Edition published in Germany

Production and Publisher: BoD – Books on Demand, Norderstedt
ISBN: 978-3-7519-9537-5

For you who stole my heart and never gave it back.

For you who stole my heart and never gave it back
I want to kiss you, want to embrace you
want to feel you.
There are thousand things I'd do but
there's this thing holding me back –
holding me from you.
And it's the fact you stole my heart and
decided to never give it back to me or
even taking care of it properly.

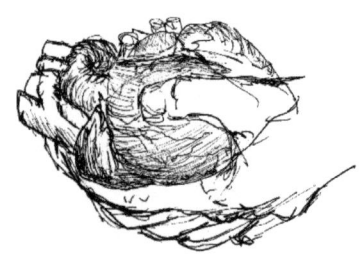

Sometimes it's love
that unites us.
But sometimes this love
pulls us apart –
it destroys us,
makes us feel lonely.
It can give us warmth
but be so cold at the same time.
Joy it is,
but sadness as well.
Oh, what a mighty thing it is
and I keep asking myself:
Oh, love, mighty love,
why do I love you so much?
Why do I love you?
Why do I use you?
I keep on going with you
even though you,
dear mighty love,
tend to hurt me.

My heartbeat's low
when you're not there.
But every slightest thought
about you makes my
heart racing.
As if I were chasing you.
As if I were following you.

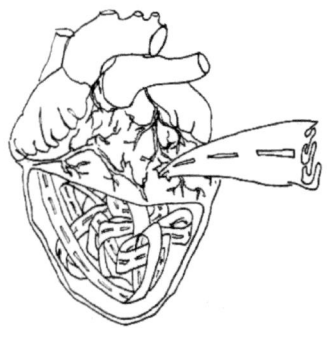

We're meant to go up,
reach the highest stars!
Stand amongst the best
and smile the brightest.
But still –
we chose to stay here,
not to reach the stars –
'cause everything we ever wanted
everything that made us smile,
was right in front of us.

Lately,
I thought about you –
in my dreams, you were there but
when waking up –
you were still gone.

All those mighty things
keep me away from you.
They make me a mess –
I feel embarrassed and
want to hide myself
in this fantasy,
the beautiful place in my dreams
where you're around and
keep me safe from all the nightmares.

Sleep safe my darling,
even though fire's around us.
Just close your eyes
and forget ...
Forget the war around us,
be safe and sound.
We might not wake up,
might not see tomorrow –
but still:
our love will keep
our souls alive ...
Alive forever
in eternity.

Just imagine it
the light in the dark
the stars in the sky
the love in our hearts

Just imagine it
wonders everywhere you go
rainbows wherever you look
fairies dancing around you

Just imagine it
this magical garden
the beauty of moonshine
you, in the middle of it

Just imagine it
me by your side
fireflies showing us the way

Our love in eternity

Sleep well, my darling.
I'll be back in the morning –
by your side.
Watching over you
to keep you safe and sound.

Let me win your heart.
Let me in your forest of darkness –
and put my light in there.
Let me love you.
Just let me in,
let me fix the broken wings of your butterflies,
butterflies of broken wings.
Just let me help you,
please, I beg you:
Let me love you.

Darkness –
it overcomes me at night.
When I can't sleep,
I stare at the ceiling and
then they come in.
Dark thoughts –
playing with my mind.
Tears in my eyes,
I start feeling alone.
Darkness overcomes me …
… and it stays.

We should finish what we started,
do all the things we came for.
We should never stop dreaming and
keep on living our dreams.
Just cut away this forest of darkness –
replace it by forests of joy and light.
We should throw away everything toxic
and only keep flowers of beauty.

Hold me close,
never let me go …
Just don't throw away
my heart of paper.
Keep it to yourself –
Keep it to your heart.

It's this state.
It makes me crazy,
but happy at the same time.
It lets me think about you,
only you, baby …
It drives me crazy,
but I like it –
just as much as I like you.

Hidden dreams.
Lost thoughts.
Fairytale around us.
Something that
unites us, but
pulls us apart at the same time.
Flying birds
surrounding us.
Heaven's right there,
rainbows in the sky.
I take my last breath,
Stop
And say goodbye.

Happy endings.
Something we all wish for.
Sometimes we get them –
sometimes we don't.
A loop we're caught in –
a vicious circle.
Love's the only way out
but the only thing I don't have.

Fireflies and flames.
High we go,
dancing around them.
Lost in our dreams –
lost in hope for love.

Tears fall,
laughter spills.
I start flying –
so high.
I fall down –
even faster.
And it repeats …
… again, and again.

My love,
stop right there.
Don't you run away,
please turn around.
Look at me.
Directly into my eyes.
Hold your breath for a moment
and now tell me you don't love me anymore.

I'm an angel –
with broken wings.
Fallen angel,
some say.
But what if I'm not fallen?
What if
I'm just in love and
broke my wings?
What if
I sacrificed everything to be
down here,
on earth?
What if –
What if it was like that?
Am I still fallen?
Just because I
sacrificed everything I had for
that one person I love?
Do you still consider me
as this fallen angel or
am I just an angel
with broken wings?

We thought we were free.
Free from everything.
Turns out
we've been wrong all the time.
We never were free.
We just escaped that one cage
to find ourselves in another one.
Caught again.
We try to escape – we make it and
find ourselves again
and again, in a new cage.
Our wings were never meant
to make us fly.
They're just here to give us hope-
Hope we now have lost –
forever!

This hate, this love, this everything.
Overwhelming me, crushing me,
pulling me down!
I'm lying there, trying to get up –
but I can't …
… everything's too much.

Stop waiting for miracles.
Do something.
Get your life in your own hands –
stop relying on others,
do your own thing.
Just don't wait for
a miracle to happen.
It can take a lifetime or
forever!
You'll regret waiting for something
that was never really meant to be.

Meant to be.
That's what I thought when
I first saw you.
I thought:
'We are meant to be!'
Turns out I was wrong –
turns out you were
meant to be with him.

Straight, gay, whatever –
labels aren't what makes us human.
It's just something, someone made up –
to feel better?
I don't know …
What makes us human
are those feelings.
It's the inside that matters.
Not only to me, but to everyone …
… even though most of us
aren't willing to admit it.

Keep those tears away from me.
Once I was drowning in them –
but now?
Now I'm free and
there's nothing left to cry about.
There are only things left to
make me happy to
give me that fulfilling life.

Cold flesh in
my ice-cold heart.
Reaching out for you.
Hands – when they touch,
spreading all the anger.
The desperate feeling of
all this hate.
The wish to finish everything –
scream and shout,
let everything out of that mind.
It leaves me desperate,
leaves you desperate,
us both desperate …
… this cold flesh,
reaching out for you
in my ice-cold heart of stone.

Sky's not the limit.
We reach higher –
want to go up.
Touch the stars and
never come back again.

Following those footsteps
deep in sand.
Having that smell in my nose
telling me where you went,
Reaching that house of stone and
realising you're not there.
Cold ashes, dust in every corner –
on every book.
You're gone now and I know –
deep in my heart –
you're never coming back …
you'll never come back,
never come back ever!

Our bodies move …
in this rhythm,
keeping us alive.
We go side by side and
I like it.
The rhythm keeps us awake,
keeps us together and
it's still keeping us alive –
even though we don't want it to.

I'm still awake.
Laying here,
right by your side.
I keep on dreaming and
wake up screaming.
Pillow in my mouth –
just don't want to wake you up.
Tears stream down my eyes.
I stay quiet –
don't say anything,
won't say anything at all.

Joy.
Happiness.
Things I want.
Tears.
Sadness.
Everything I get.
I keep asking myself:
Why, baby? Why?

Those green eyes –
I'm obsessed.
Closing my eyes,
instantly seeing them.
Having your face
in my mind.
Each expression caught
like the finest photograph.
Those butterflies,
they keep on flying –
keep on telling me about you.
That desire
getting bigger and bigger.
The smile on my face
becoming wider the more I see you.
Everything seems so gorgeous –
and when you're here
rainbow fairies take over and
I'm overwhelmed.

Stone cold,
they call me.
But I –
I really don't care.
I keep breathing,
keep living and
pretend as if
nothing happened.
But then
those moments come,
when everything gets dark.
Everything seems to swallow me –
it inhales me.
And suddenly:
I start to care.
Tears stream down my face and
I stop pretending.
Stop pretending as if
nothing happened.
I start to care and,
guess what,
it destroys me.
I'm not dead, but half alive.

The day of roses,
the day of love.
Red roses everywhere –
love is in the air.
But isn't it absurd,
that, suddenly,
one day decides
how everything will end …

So dreamy,
so wonderful.
I wish I could
be with you.

The way I went
to find you …
so much distance
to get to you …
and then
you just walked away.

Sometimes we love,
sometimes we hate.
In moments we wish to disappear,
in moments we wish to be there.
I want to love you.
I want to hate you – sometimes.
Maybe I wish to disappear, but –
mostly I wish to be there …
to be there with you,
to be there by your side.

Some things never fade away,
won't ever fade away, go away-
Like our love –
even when we're gone,
it'll be there for eternity.

Don't close your eyes.
Look at it!
Face the truth – reality.
Don't get caught up
in those unrealistic dreams.
Don't stop dreaming at altogether.

Make those feelings go away,
I don't want them anymore.
I wish to fly away,
make them miss me even more.

Day whatever of feeling empty.
Inside …
All those demons …
Make them go away,
Burn them in hell,
So, no one can tell
It was me.

In my wildest dreams
I could never
think of
drinking that coffee
with you in Paris.

Oh Paris,
city of love,
you're in my head,
in my mind.
Oh Paris,
show me your beauty,
I'll give you my love.
Oh Paris,
my beloved Paris,
why do I love thee so much?
why can't I let go of thee?
Oh Paris,
dear Paris,
you fill up my senses,
I can't live without you …
can't breathe without you.

Skinny dipping
With you at night.
Lulled by moonshine,
Just you and me.
Our bodies:
Tight.
Sweet cherry lips,
Smile on your face.
Kiss me,
Embrace me,
Fill me.
I want to
Taste that
Bittersweet
Feeling of your love.

And maybe we'll just need
This little sparkle to tell us:
It's all going to be alright.

Your soft squishy lips,
Your rough cheek.
Those dimples and
Green dreamy eyes,
Your smile that
Let's me melt away.
Me wanting you by my side
Is all I desire.

Can you see her
Lying in
This sea of stars?
Unable to see them in
Her night gown
Floating with the wind.
Her body so fragile
So broken but
Strong at the same time.
I wanna kiss her,
Feel her in my arms,
Help her see those stars,
Help her see the light in this world.

Sing me to sleep
With this lullaby
I wanna see your face
Feel your lips
When you kiss me goodnight.

Kiss me.
Hate me.
Embrace me.
Enrage me.
Just do anything.
Don't just stand there
Staring and watching.

For you who stole my heart:
let me steal yours too.
Let us be tangled in those sheets
all night long …
all day long …
just forever.
Kiss until we can't breathe and
blow each other's minds away until the end of days.

Just realised
how fucked up
our lives are
and that
there will be no us.
Just you and I
going separate ways.

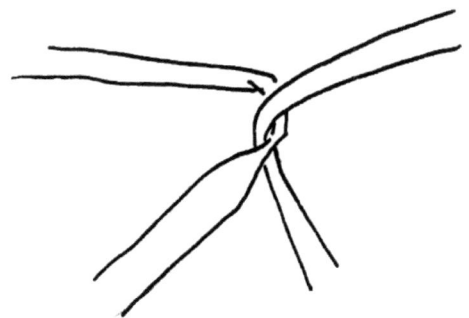

Stripping there naked
underneath the dark blue sky
surrounded by this black water
yeah, you and me
alone in the Seine
alone in Paris.

Drink with me
that glass of wine,
we'll have a chat
all night long
'bout life, 'bout love,
'bout everything.

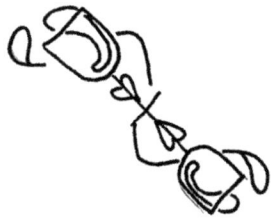

Hang on, baby.
Stay for a last kiss,
or even more?

Lacey pieces
covering the smallest parts.
Our eyes meet,
you smile and
come near for this
first kiss.

When I said yes to
drinking that coffee
with you in Paris,
I never thought
ending up with
this glass of red wine
in our bed.

Her skin
of porcelain,
her lips like
red, red wine.
Oh, what would I give,
for one night
in her arms.

Seduced
is what I felt when
I tasted those
cherry lips,
put my arms
around those
defined lines.

When he gave me his hand,
I took it and
along came
this bittersweet
taste of surrender.

Blurry faces,
moving houses.
Guess, I'm drunk.
So drunk to tell
that I love you.

It's time to dance on tables and drink out of bellies.
It's time to let ourselves go and
enjoy this short time we were given.

I refuse
to die
when not
by your side.

Life put you
out there
for me
to find you.

Sunburned kisses
is what we get and
the thing we dream
about
all night long.

When I said
everything was fine I
somehow didn't mean it –
what I meant was
to say that
I'm broken, I'm lost, I'm down and
I can't do all of this anymore.
When I said
all was fine
between you and me, us,
I didn't mean it –
I wanted to say that
I fell in love with you and
that I can't see her in your arms.

Sitting in his lap with
a cherry in her mouth.
She leans over,
whispers in his ear and
starts to laugh.
Soft laughter
followed by
cool-warm kisses.

Fucked up.
Two words that
mean a world.
I feel this way.
You do.
They do.
We do.

I hate it
when you're
not there.
When you're
with him and
not by my side.

What's so wrong with this word …
… *love* they call it.
They adore it and
it tears them apart.
Still –
they fall for it.
I stand here watching,
hating it, wanting it to burn!
And in the end –
in the end I keep coming back
adoring it.

'Cause we're six feet under –
so deep, so skin deep.

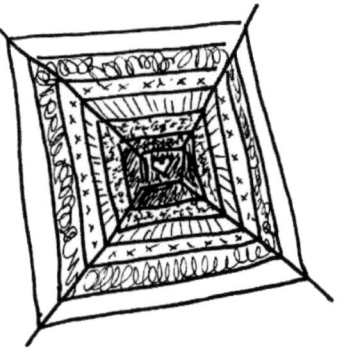

Her tiny figure
in that moonlight water.
That barely covered body,
soft pearls dripping down her chest,
driving me crazy.
My hands –
longing to be everywhere.
Everything
taking away my breath.
Feels like I was
drowning while still being alive.

Let it rain on us,
this water of joy,
flames of lust and
earth of desire.
Let me embrace you
be tangled up in
your mighty sheets,
surrounded by
your lovely scent that
feels like pheromones
attracting me.

Striped t-shirt –
I put it off me.
What is left is bare skin.
One step forward and
I reach the ice-cold water.
Does it matter?
No, not at all.
Though cold, warmth spreads
Through my body.
Your presence takes away
All the pressure.
What is left are
Our bodies together and
The field of desire
Surrounding us.

Let thoughts flow
And before they show
You must know
It wasn't all
For your damn fall
So get out and stop to crawl.
You're more than this.
You can keep controlling this.

It's time to lay down,
Here, in this mighty place,
right next to you.
Why, you ask?
Because I'm about to drown,
want you to keep safe,
feel your love through and through.
It's your right to ask, to
ask me anything when
you lie next to me.
It's time to set your feelings free –
set them free, let them be,
even though they're hidden deep dark.
Why, you want to know?
Because I'm able to see
what's deep inside, so let it be me,
you show your feelings too – I'm not afraid of the dark,
if that's what you want to know.
All the darkness already took me,
but I threw back my light.

Does it even matter what we think,
what we feel and what we dream about?
What we desire and what we want?
That's your question.
My answer is: it does, otherwise we'll sink
into this deep darkness and forget to be loud.
To be ourselves and really show what we want.
You can ask whatever question you
want to ask me and
I'll always have an answer for you.

Shades do wander at night, don't they?
Light's only there where the sun is and
love only follows the ones deserving it.
These are statements you make.
Shades wander – no matter what time – their way
and light's always there, even in your tiny hand.
Love follows everyone which means everyone deserves it?
Ask yourself this question or even
ask yourself:
why shouldn't everyone deserve love?

Sand from the beach and
all that salty water.
You and me in the waves
together – our hair wet and
bodies together.
Walking down this path and
ending up in the shower,
yeah, you and me.
The warm, warm water
touching our skin and
us laughing together.
When we finally feel
the soft, cold sheets beneath us
the sun has already set.
Night has begun and
between us this little play of joy
in this hotel room in Spain.

Bare skin is
what was left behind
those empty doors of
treasure.
When you took
everything of me
I thought it was nothing.
Never imagined
you would let me fall –
fall so hard.
In this empty, cruel world,
this destroyed, evil world,
this world full of loneliness.

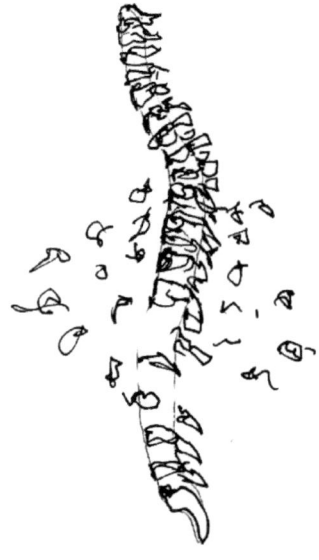

There was a time
A time we were safe.
Yeah, you and I
When I lay there
In your arms
In this comfy place …
My lips, red and swollen like
Sweet cherries you plucked
From your backyard.
Our eyes meeting and
Being lost.
There was this time but
Now it is no more.
Give me space
Keep me safe
I said.
But what you did was
Give me space and
Not keep me safe.

Show me the stars, baby.
Even if we can't reach them
We still see them.
'Cause it's the distance that
Shows us how
Much they mean to us.

We were burning
With all this passion –
Us together
And then –
It all fell apart
Suddenly with
No warning.
It just
Fell
apart.

Bare skin, ripped jeans,
Blood on hands, empty corpses.
All the light – it's
Fading away …
I collapse, fall –
So deep
Till I hit the hard, hard ground.
Eyes closed, hands tied
Waiting for
Them to come,
Some last words
By a stranger trying to
Comfort me but
Bringing up that anger
That anger that's been there forever.
The clock strikes midnight,
A death cry shattering the darkness and then:
Silence.
Sweet and lovely silence.

Sleepless nights
Thinking about you.
My thoughts circle and circle –
On and on all the time.
Your stunning eyes in my head,
These dimples in front of
My closed eyes.
I can't help it,
Wish I could or wait:
I don't.
I like them, those
Sleepless nights
Thinking about you.

Lying awake at night
And thinking about those moments,
The ones we had together in Paris.
Thinking of that coffee at Montmartre.
Lying in those sheets.
Glasses of red, red wine in our hands.
Our hearts glowing of passion,
Looking through the window and
Seeing those city lights far away.
It was just the two of us.
I remember those moments, at night.
Those nights we had …
A smile comes upon my face
And then I think of that one moment …
I wish you had never let me go.

Darkness overcomes me.
Pure darkness …
and the light –
all gone.
All what's left are
the embers of
that huge fire that used to
flare and bring light to
every tiny corner.

Burn in hell,
she thought,
but didn't realise that
he would have been
the one
to help her out
this hole of darkness …
… even though he was the one,
who dug the first foot.

Be wild,
be free,
be with me.
In Paris,
the city of love,
of burning passion,
where we'll make love and
our souls connect for eternity.

Her silhouette
driving me crazy.
Her standing in the Seine,
moonshine on her body,
water flowing along her lines.
Oh, I'm just a man,
so crazy in love,
wanting to embrace her,
wanting to feel something,
wanting to feel the best,
wanting to feel her wanted.

Take me to Paris.
I'll burn in the flames of passion,
walk in the fields of desire and
end up
winded up in your arms.
With only you by my side,
I'll walk, I'll talk.
Your hands keep me safe,
protect me from harm.
And in Paris, we'll give this all a name …
Just take me to Paris.

One more cup of coffee.
For me and you.
In that café.
in Paris,
where we first met,
where we first fell in love.

When she said one more,
she meant the coffee
and not
ending up in those sheets
with that glass of red, red wine
and her red, red lips
teasing his
delicate neck.

Dark, but full moon,
when we went skinny dipping
in that lake somewhere in
the nowhere or
was it near Paris?
Memory's blurred.
I see your laughing face –
so close, so close to mine – and
I have those feelings,
the feelings I'll never forget.
Ever.

I admit,
I was rude, ignored you.
Didn't even greet you.
Acted like I didn't see you –
but I did. I noticed you.
All the time.
I was hurt.
That's the reason why.
That's the reason why I did that,
acted this way, ignored you.
I was hurt, so deep inside.
Hurt, 'cause I liked you and you
didn't like me back.
It's not your fault, is it?
You can't like everyone, can you?
Sounds like I was mad at you
for not liking me.
But I'm not.
Not at you, rather at myself –
for liking you.
I hate this feeling, of liking you,
but then,
I love it. I want to keep this feeling and
talking to you makes it worse.
Worse than before.
I hope, you understand.
Understand the way I acted and
I really do,
I admit it.

We're burning bridges down
and they burn, burn, burn ...
The heat feels like our love,
so good, but repulsive at the same time.
This anger inside me –
blazing like hell.
I'll burn more and more and more –
with or without you –
until they blast.
I come to rest,
in those cold-warm ashes,
those soft and shimmery ashes
showing that all is gone and
new is to come.

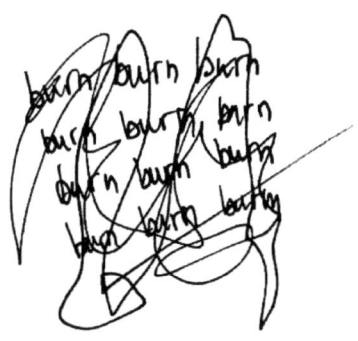

And maybe we're all fucked up people,
with fucked up minds,
in this fucked up world.

Maybe we're crazy,
with crazy minds,
in a crazy world.

Some say, we're survivors,
having surviving minds,
for a surviving world.

But what about being saviours?
Or just being normal?
I guess that's not what we are,
what we never were and
what we'll never be.

Sleepover in your bed
and having you in my head,
all night, all dreams.
Waking up next to you feels like
seeing the sunrise in the arctic after
long, long darkness.
Those tangled sheets and
spilled drops of red wine from last night …
Smile on my face.
Watching you breathe while
the sun rises over Paris and
birds start singing.
Your green eyes open and meet mine.
That smile on your face showing off
those tiny, lovely dimples.
You pull me close and we kiss.
Pull me closer, I think.
And you do.
We get tangled up in sheets again
before we have that coffee and
my favourite pains au chocolat …
Yeah, those sleepovers in your bed.

Kiss me baby,
until the sun rises,
until we're united again,
until the moon reaches the sun.

Hold me close
until morning comes and
all the stars collide;
until everything collides.

Embrace me
until we reach the sky and
then fall, fall so deep,
until we hit the hard-soft ground.

Let me lie by your side,
until the world falls apart,
until everything we know is gone,
until there's nothing left for us to be.

And then, finally,
let our souls unite;
in this broken world where
the only thing we'll ever have is each other.

When I see you,
I think of Paris.
The city of love –
which brought so much pain
in my vein
and all that rain.
Sitting in the train
crying all those tears
on my way home.
I think about the time we had.
Romantic, beautiful, passionate.
Before the day you broke my heart,
the day you broke my soul –
this dark day, when rain fell,
and never stopped.
When I see you,
I relive this moment.
When I hear 'Paris',
I'm thrown back to that time.
Wish I could forget,
make new memories –
without you.
Sometimes I even wish
I had never met you.
But then I think:
Without you I would have never grown that strong.

Sometimes we feel lost
in this soft bliss of misery …
created through love –
I guess?

Drops of blood
dripping, tipping, tapping …
Oh sweet, sweet life
of red, red rose,
your thorns like love and
sweet, sweet life dripping away.

My thoughts wander –
only around you, my love.
Your lovely green eyes
resembling shimmering emeralds.
Lips of honey tasting
sugary, bitterly sweet.
What would I give, my dear,
to spend that lovely night
with you, oh honey.
What would I give
for one last kiss –
under the moonlight –
at our favourite place in Paris.

My mind wanders,
wanders around and around and around.
This feeling overcomes me
and makes me –
I feel empty.
A single tear …
… fading into a river.
Is this what falling feels like?
The wind around my face,
Twirling my hair and …
… this freedom!
Until the hard ground comes,
until reality faces me.
Suddenly I'm small again.
Darkness overcomes me
and brings along emptiness.

Never thought that
loving someone
would mean hurting.
Hurting so bad and
crying yourself to sleep.
Sleep fulfilled with
bittersweet nightmares.
Nightmares that would
come true and bring you to an end.
End, end, end …
… E-N-D …
… this bitter-cruel end.

I admit it,
I feel empty.
So what?

Is it just me or
do you feel it too?
This emptiness that
swallows everything …
… everything.

Kiss me under the moonlight.
under the tree
where we first met and
left our sign of love.
At the edge of Paris,
with a coffee and
pain au chocolat in our hands.
The crumbs on your dimples,
my gentle hands swiping them away.
Your lovely, charming smile
and my lips that kiss you goodbye.

And sometimes
this emptiness overcomes me.
Emptiness, darkness …
whether I'm alive or not –
time will decide.
Once he said:
'Just feel your heartbeat
and you'll know you're alive.'
It keeps on beating,
keeping me alive.
But what if
I'm dead inside?
What if
the person I used to be
is gone?
What if, what if, what if …
I just want to feel something.
Even if it's this blade in my skin.

About life and death.
They come and go,
are bright and fade away.
One day we'll fade away too.
But for now: why don't we just bloom?

The blue, blue sky is what I like,
she said.
It lets me escape,
from reality, from everything that's
on my mind, on my heart.
Suddenly I forget everything and
this tiny cloud tells me:
Everything will be okay.

Dancing around in their pure beauty
telling us that
working together is
what makes the impact.
Maybe we should do it as well,
work together and
leave this loneliness behind us.

Let me out,
out, out, out …
Wish I was free, but
this biding spell is holding me back.
Back from life, back from love,
back from almost everything?
It's getting loud,
loud, loud, loud …
Maybe I should go up
where nothing can stop me, 'cause
there's no lack.
Lack of life, lack of love,
lack of almost everything?
I could be proud,
proud, proud, proud …
Not constantly pushing this sack.
Sack full of life, sack full of love,
sack full of almost everything?
Or maybe I just need help,
or even rest.
Help from anyone,
rest from anything?

Maybe the thing that hurt me the most
was my love for you.
All this desire to be with you,
to feel your affection, to feel your love
was just an imaginary fantasy and
all the time it was never meant to be.

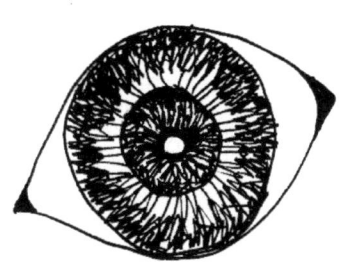

What I feel is empty.
Try to hide it
but I fail.
That shine in my eyes:
gone.
Replaced with
this empty look.
Empty and sad
Even though
all I wanted was love.

One day you'll be over her
able to laugh 'bout these moments ...
The moments you both had together,
enjoyed – when you laughed and
she lay there in your arms.
Her brown eyes and warm smile,
all those memories
driving you crazy.
But one day you'll be over her, boy.

Why do I keep loving you?
Why, oh why?
Wish I could let go –
you go or
maybe everything?
But I wanna keep loving you,
don't let go of those feelings –
maybe never let go of you?
Wish I could forget, but then –
I don't want to forget,
forget you ...
what you made me feel like.
Never ever, never ever ...
It'll keep on killing me and
I'll maybe keep on crying myself to sleep-
But all I wanna do is love you.

When snow's falling
and lights are shining –
the smell of cinnamon
all around – everywhere.
Christmas songs playing,
laughter in the air!
Smiling faces,
the most beautiful time of the year!
Come and dance with me,
sing with me
under this beautiful tree.

Let's fall in love and
forget about everything –
'bout everything around us …
Let's think about us and
stop being friends.
Let's be lovers all along.
Come and let passion find us,
embrace us.
Let's set our minds free,
let's be free …
Free from everything,
even love?

How dying would feel right now –
I don't know …
don't ask me.
When I haven't experienced …
how could I tell.
Do I want to tell?
I wish I could.
How it would feel,
blood running down my fingers.
My throat red, bloody red.
I would want to know
how it feels …
Tell how's it feel.
Should I try, try, try …
Oh, why, why, why …
My, my, my …
Just go away …
chaos in my head.

Please like me.
Not the way
you like your neighbour or
your dog.
More like liking your one,
your person. The one
you want to be with.
But I don't want drama,
nor forced feelings.
I just want you
to like me the way I am,
to lay beside me and
smile, so I can smile back.

Kinda hate this feeling,
when you're not there.
Lovely dimples and
Green, green eyes …
I could get lost –
lost and then be found.
Found by you, dear,
only you.
Your presence driving me crazy but
fulfilling at the same time.
When you're not there I
feel lost. Lost in this forest of
dark and twisty creatures.
And when you're there, I'll
easily find the path of redemption.

I might leave everything behind –
this world, you, even me.
What love means to me?
I don't know.
I might know many things,
but this one thing I can't seem to know.
Feels like it fell to me,
flew to me, caught me up?
What I know is this feeling,
feeling of missing you …
… sometimes even crying in my misery.

Both of them wandering my mind.
Big brown eyes and skin soft like caramel.
That's her.
In her true beauty.
Her laugh – music in my ears,
feels like perfection.
Still, I see her. And it hurts. So badly.
Feel like crawling in my bed.
The other one –
understanding me the way I am-
I look at our memories and wish,
wish I could finally tell her.
'Bout how I feel, 'bout how
she makes me feel.
Her eyes of soft brown kind.
Both wandering my mind.
Is it love?
But still, if it wasn't, it'd still feel breath-taking.
When the one's not in my head,
the other indeed is …
Confused by love, or whatever this feeling is,
I wander the world.
Wander around, wonder around,
constantly thinking about May or Day.
Will it ever stop?
I don't know or
maybe I don't want to know.

Kiss me before I go, babe.
One last kiss, before I leave, boy.
That smile on your face,
showing dimples.
If it were so simple.
Hold me before I go.
Your hand in mine and
mine in yours.
Our foreheads touching.
Wish I could have told you –
so much!
So much and everything
before I left and never returned.
And never will I return,
watching you from above.
But the smile's gone,
rather a frown.
Wish I could tell you,
that I'm always by your side.
If it was up to me,
everything would be different.
Still –
one thing would stay the same:
I would have always saved you.

I know you like that somebody.
The one with those
pretty eyes, amazing hair.
The one with this
lovely, pretty smile
being so sweet and bubbly
all the time.
But maybe,
maybe I like you too.
The way you like that one.
You were here with that somebody –
at least with your mind –
when I saw you on that Tuesday.
We were sitting, chatting together,
'bout life, 'bout stud, 'bout kinda everything.
Your eyes show that depth.
Your smile is that lovely, pretty smile for me
being so sweet and bubbly.
The way of teasing makes me feel …
… feel alive …
But I know you like that somebody.
That somebody I'll never be.

The void inside
spreading sadness.
Empty promises, empty eyes.
Wake up, wake up!
Avoid the outside,
leaving this world full of …
… beauty they say …
… or as I call it:
the land of empty promises.

You don't own me.
Neither do I own you.
Still, I'd like to call you mine and
hope you'll call me yours too.
Hand in hand we'll go,
see this bright, new world,
discover the strangest places.
Smiles on our faces,
laughter in our minds.
Love is in the air,
they'd say.
But haven't I realised yet that
all I wish for
is long gone …
… faded away for too long.
Still, I'd like to call you mine anyway
though you're long gone.
Far, far away.
All you left are those traces.
Traces leading back to me.
Traces torturing me.

When I was thinking about you,
in the middle of the night:
I was wide awake,
wide awake lying there,
crying me eyes out.
Heart aching,
tears streaming,
thoughts flying –
far, far away.
Wish you were here,
right by my side.

Tell me pretty lies, dear.
I'll believe you.
Eyes closed,
open heart.
I'm just a fool,
believing you,
loving you,
adoring you.
I hope you care.
I don't.
Don't care anymore,
'bout whether you
truly love me
or not,
whether everything's fake
or not.
These feelings
drive me crazy,
and the only thing I care about
are my foolish feelings for you.

We don't
always get
what we
desire
but maybe
we should inspire
now or
not quite yet.

ask yourself:
where am I?
what am I?
who am I?
or even
ask yourself:
am I?

Dream.
Stop.
Scream.
Stop.
Shout.
Stop.
Out. Stop.
Keep on dreaming,
don't you stop.
With that screaming
you have to stop.
Shouting, not necessary,
just stop.
I'll be out
and never stop.

No, they said.
No, I was told.
No, was the word.
No – just a phrase.
No, I don't want to.
No was what I
didn't want to hear.
No, everyone screamed.
No, no, no, no!
Now is what I want!

Your friends tell you to hate me,
but you still keep on loving me.
Just tell me why, girl,
Why do you keep loving me?
Even though I keep messing up …

                              Close your eyes
                    we'll leave everything behind
                                    and in the end
                              it's just you and me
                                falling in love.

Even if the
brightest star
burns out tonight
I'll still follow you,
go wherever you go,
win your heart and
love you for eternity.

Is it just me?
Me – who
overthinks
and
overthinks
over and over
and over
again …
Or is there
someone
else as well?

DON'T FORGET
I WON'T FORGET
WE WON'T FORGET:
WHAT YOU'VE
DONE,
DONE TO ME,
DONE TO MY HEART.

Maybe I just wanted
all your love.

Let us fall,
fall in love …
even if it's not simple –
let's try …
just you and me.

It's not only
me who fell
for you that day.
It wasn't only
my heart …
it was my soul –
my soul and
each and every
part of me.

Crazy creative, crazy obsessed …
Obsessed by love, love and music,
music and love.

Isn't it ironic
Those things we long for
The people we love
Everything
One day all of this
Will fall apart

                              It doesn't have to be –
                              be this certain way …
                              unless you want to.
                                     Do you?
                                'Cause I don't.
                              I don't want us to
                                         change
                              I don't want us to
                              fully fall apart.

Keep me safe, keep me safe,
keep me all along by your side.
I'm not brave, not really brave,
but I'll go with you on that ride.
That ride of joy all by your side,
just promise me once again:
Promise to keep me safe.

Can't stop thinking about you.
The ways you tease me and
the way you laugh …
but I shouldn't think this way 'cause –
it would ruin everything and
it would change the way we interact.
I guess you'd stop teasing me or
even stop talking to me.

I'm so confused.
Can't stop
thinking about you.
Can I call it love
or is it
just friendship?

Let me share those experiences
with you, my darling.
Embrace me, hold me close and
when you kiss me
don't forget:
hold on tight, baby.
'Cause I love you and I love you …
… and I love you.

For that person who turned out to be a
useless prick – just go away,
can't you do me this favour?
Kangaroos out of plush won't help either,
your time has passed, honey.
Oh, just leave me because you don't even
understand what you did to me!

We should stop pretending,
actually, we should've
done it earlier …
way earlier …
… why, you ask?
'Cause it's wrong,
it always has been and
it always will be …

We kiss, then we cry,
we kiss and cry –
over and over again.
Your lips on mine, …
… our tongues dancing with
each other and
our hearts beating synchronically.
Tears streaming down our
faces – us crying –
it hurts, but we still
keep on going.
Keep on kissing and crying.
It hurts but
still is the best feeling on this world.

Green shimmering eyes following
my mind and sometimes even
making me go crazy like
a lost wanderer in the garden of Eden.
Those dimples with this
charming smile make feel
welcome and loved and even
charmed like the long-lost princess in
her magic castle on a faraway kingdom.
The way he acts, walks and talks reminds
me of the things I love
to do, the things that
make me feel home and safe.
I just wish he would notice
me and the way I feel and
all the things I do to
make him notice me and
notice that I not only like him but
that I fall for him.

What love feels like?
It feels different for
each and everyone out there.
But for me?
For me it is butterflies and strawberries,
sweet cherries and
red, red roses.
Mighty it is,
makes me go crazy
and not think with my mind –
but with my heart.
It feels like my
happy place,
happy place on earth which
then seems to be everywhere.

My secret admiration for you,
it's there, but you
don't see it 'cause
I won't let you see.
I'll keep it secret and
maybe it's perfect this way.
Maybe this secret admiration
is what I hold on to,
hold on when I
think about you,
you and the world.

Won't let you down
won't let me down,
us down, no one down.
If you just closed
your eyes and
believed, believed in all
those fairy tales.
If you just did …
… but you don't.

Don't lie to me,
come and lie with me.
Dare to open your eyes,
don't hesitate to close them.
Come closer and closer and closer –
until bodies touch,
until souls unite,
until night reaches day and
day reaches night.
Don't you hesitate to
wake me up and
don't you hesitate to
tell me about your deepest fears.
I'll be there, I'll be there,
right by your side to
comfort you and keep you safe.

Kiss me before I go,
before I leave,
leave this city of love,
this city of passion,
where our hearts joined.
Kiss me
one last time,
one last time in Paris,
oui, à Paris, mon amour!

We're crazy
in love
sipping coffee
all the way to
Paris
waiting for
our dreams to
finally come
true.

I lay awake,
all night,
all morning,
all time …
thinking about you,
'bout love, 'bout everything …
especially 'bout
our time together –
together in Paris!

She ran
from love
even though
it saved her.

I am not
sorry.
'Bout what
I did.
'Cause I
just loved.
Unless it is
a crime,
you can't
blame me.

Keep me safe
and save
me from the night.

If you're reading this
I'm in love with you, baby –
so deeply, truly in love …
I keep listening to the same songs
over and over again,
to your favourite song
over and over again:
just to have that one piece of you
even though –
even though you don't know –
of how much I love you …
it kills me from the inside
and I can't and won't help it,
'cause I'm deeply, truly in love with you.

One day you'll be over her –
over those memories and
her big brown eyes.
Eventually it'll fade away …
… all those memories and
you'll be happier boy!
One day you'll look back –
you'll laugh and maybe,
maybe you'll thank her.
You still love her, but you'll
never hate her …
The memories and moments
with her never seem
to leave you, boy –
but remember:
it'll fade away and be a distant memory …
Yeah, one day, boy, you'll be over her.

If I die –
I want you to be by my side,
holding my hand 'til,
'til I take my last breath.
Woven eyes, fallen skies.
One last taste of your lips –
tastes cotton candy sweet.
The smile on your face,
one last time for me to see.
Wish you were not gone,
gone so far, far away –
just to find your own way.
Wish you were here.
Right by my side.
'Cause it feels like I'm dying without you.

Acknowledgements

This one's for all the Ladies and Fellas out there, who've loved with all their heart. For those, who've been heartbroken. For those who don't even believe in love. Just for everyone out there.

Oh, and if you're reading this, yes, I mean YOU, then I'm thanking you. Why? Because you're reading this, and it means a lot to me!

And what's up with that title? Is it for someone specific? Well, let's just keep these questions open. Maybe I'll answer them one day …

By the way, these little illustrations aren't by me as you might have noticed. They're by Julia Hann von Weyhern. Thank you so much for them! This book wouldn't look the way it looks now without you.

Oh yeah, and thanks to Isabel Grevenstein and Roman Hambrecht for finding all my mistakes and commenting everything to make editing fun. I owe you a lot!

Thanks to Emilie Pfeffer, Anna Vodopjanov, Nina Imgraben, Max Wolfsperger, Luca Lohmayr, Michael Dippel and Niklas Kniebühler for being the first ones to read "For you, who stole my heart". Thanks for telling how this book made you feel and thanks for all your love!

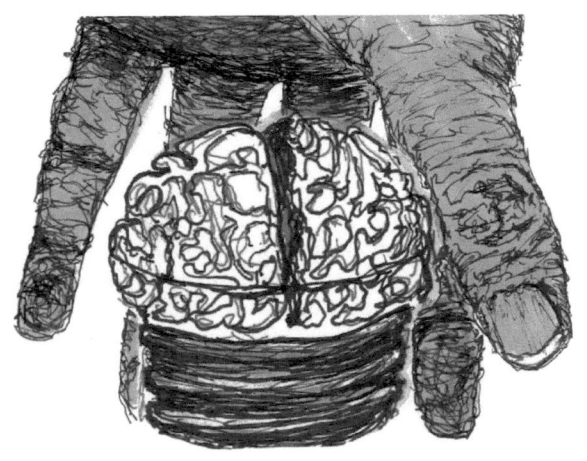